CULTIVATING EARLY READING DEVELOPMENT:
Reaping the Benefits of School Success!

Dr. Alvin Haywood, Ed.D.

Cultivating Early Reading Development
Reaping the Benefits of School Success!
All Rights Reserved.
Copyright © 2019 Dr. Alvin Haywood, Ed.D.
v2.0 r1.0

The opinions expressed in this manuscript are solely the opinions of the author and do not represent the opinions or thoughts of the publisher. The author has represented and warranted full ownership and/or legal right to publish all the materials in this book.

This book may not be reproduced, transmitted, or stored in whole or in part by any means, including graphic, electronic, or mechanical without the express written consent of the publisher except in the case of brief quotations embodied in critical articles and reviews.

Outskirts Press, Inc.
http://www.outskirtspress.com

ISBN: 978-1-9772-0606-0

Library of Congress Control Number: 2018913499

Cover Photo © 2019 Steven Cotton Photography. All rights reserved - used with permission.

Outskirts Press and the "OP" logo are trademarks belonging to Outskirts Press, Inc.

TABLE OF CONTENTS

1. Early Education Enrichment Experiences 1
2. Key Early Foundation Reading Skills 8
3. Understanding the Concept of Curriculum and Instruction 13
4. Kindergarten, First-, and Second-Grade Reading Instruction 16
5. Assessment 20
6. Third-Grade Reading Instruction 22
7. Reading Motivation Is Key 24
8. Fourth-Grade Transition 27
9. Eight-Step Plan for Teaching Expository Text Structures 32
10. Teaching English Language Learners 34
11. Children With Learning Disabilities 37
12. Conclusion 39
About the Author 43
References 46

INTRODUCTION

Developing and enriching a child's reading and overall literacy experiences should begin at birth. Most brain development occurs during the first three years of life. If these beginning stages of brain development are not stimulated, cultivated, and nourished, many children will have fallen academically and socially behind their peers before they start kindergarten (Kupcha-Szrom, 2011). Children need to be read to, have ongoing access to lots of books to explore and discuss, and be exposed to ongoing rich and meaningful vocabulary.

Kindergarten readiness. Since in kindergarten and first grade, reading comprehension refers more to development of phonemic awareness, word recognition skills, and listening comprehension, reading to children is one of the most important literacy activities for children (International Reading Association Common Core State Standards (CCSS) Committee, 2012; Lunenburg, 2011; Mustard, 2010). Reading aloud to children has four major benefits: 1) It improves *readiness* for school for children, 2) it instills *positive attitudes* toward reading, 3) it helps to develop *lifelong* reading habits, and 4) it develops a *love* for reading for any aged child (Lunenburg, 2011; Short, Lynch-Brown, & Tomlinson, 2014).

Four major factors that have a positive impact on kindergarten achievement are:

- Early rich and meaningful home reading experiences
- High-quality preschool experience
- Strong and meaningful parent/child interactions
- High parental expectations

It's never too early to start experiencing books.

1 EARLY EDUCATION ENRICHMENT EXPERIENCES

Preschool. There has been a growing body of research studies that reveal having a *high-quality* and *strong preschool experience* has a direct positive correlation to formal school readiness (Skolnick, Hirsh-Pasek, & Golinkoff, 2013). A high-quality preschool physical setting, curriculum, and literacy environment has a direct positive impact on the attitudes of children toward reading and writing and the resulting growth and development that takes place in those same curriculum areas (Cunningham, 2008). The overall quality of a preschool classroom's physical environment, instructional approaches, and teacher emotional support systems is associated with children's behavior and learning skill readiness for early formal schooling. In this context, *learning behaviors* are defined as a skill set of various ways children adapt and react to situations they encounter while learning, such as solving problems and collaborating with other children (Dominguez, Vitiello, Fuccillo, Greenfield & Bulotsky-Shearer, 2011). Therefore, in addition to academic curriculum areas, children who maintain good self-regulation skills, in a high-quality preschool environment, have higher academic outcomes in later formal school grades than children who had poor self-regulation skills in preschool.

Self-regulation skills are commensurate with a child's ability to maintain self-control, or the ability to remain calm, focused, thoughtful, and collaborative during direct instruction, guided play, or free play sessions (Riva & Ryan, 2015).

Developing and assessing self-regulation, and other executive function high-level cognitive skills of preschoolers, in the context of ongoing and positive *child-teacher bonds*, enhances children's collaborative engagement, attention control, language development, and later reading and math achievement (Anderson & Reidy, 2012; Commodari, 2013; Welsh, Nix, Blair, Bierman, & Nelson, 2010).

Overall, high-quality preschool experiences have a large, long-lasting and positive impact on school academic achievement, higher end-of-year preschool test scores in reading and math, the general well-being of children, increased school attendance, fewer special education placements, a decline in overall grade level retentions, and higher high school graduation rates. Also, high-quality preschool experiences result in a reduction in crime, a boost in income earnings over a lifetime, a reduced need and application for public welfare assistance, reduced childcare costs, and a positive impact on the economic returns on dollars invested.

The returns are estimated to be $4 to over $10 on each dollar invested in high-quality preschool education (Bakken,

Great books can bring out the best in you!

Brown, & Downing, 2017; Cascio & Schanzenbach, 2013; Gormley, Phillips, & Anderson, 2017; Karoly, 2017; Reynolds & Temple, 2008). Thus, one guiding principle could be that *early prevention* at the preschool level is a far better cost-effective choice than trying to make up for losses in later school years (Justice, 2006).

The value of constructive play in learning. During the first three years of life, when the brain is experiencing most of its development, and on through the preschool and early primary school grades, children need large amounts of time to engage in uninterrupted and *guided play* (Nespeca, 2012). Guided play is described as being somewhere between direct instruction and free play. Guided play takes place in a *developmentally appropriate* setting, or play learning center, where there is a purposeful learning goal. Children can then explore and exercise a majority of control over the learning experience (Nespeca, 2012; Skolnick et al., 2013).

A key *constructivist* instructional strategy to remember is that children increase their academic and social engagement when they are *actively involved* and interactive in their learning, as opposed to being passive learners. There is a *balance* of both *teacher guidance* and *open student exploration* (Pang, 2009; Sanacore & Palumbo, 2009). Learning that is playful makes room for individual differences, the mastery of concepts, and the accomplishment of learning goals (Rushton, 2011).

Pretend, or dramatic play, is well established as a way to develop literacy skills in young children, but *constructive play* also has a positive impact on the development of vocabulary and oral language skills, as well as on math achievement and a child's social-emotional development. For example, *while observing and playing with blocks and Legos*, toddlers as young as three and older engage with the same abstract symbols of shape and form that are needed for *visual discrimination* of letters and word formations that stand for words and concepts. During constructive play, children can be encouraged to *talk about* what they are building, work together, and learn new words in the process (Nespeca, 2012; Sussman, 2012).

Early vocabulary and comprehension development. When rich and meaningful home/preschool vocabulary development takes place in the earliest years, the more of a critical advantage that child has over those children who do not receive early verbal, vocabulary, and other reading experiences (Wasserman, 2007).

Vocabulary is crucial in developing reading skills (Hart & Risley, 1995). Vocabulary development not only aids in reading comprehension, but vocabulary also helps in the development of writing (Graham, MacArthur, & Fitzgerald, 2013; Robinson, McKenna, & Conradi, 2012). Conversely, instruction in writing improves word reading and reading fluency. Also, writing about what one has read improves comprehension of that reading material (Graham & Hebert, 2011). Using both reading and writing exercises helps children understand and make connections among subject-matter components, especially when they are engaged with informational text (McKeown, Beck, & Blake, 2009).

Oral language and literacy development work and grow together side-by-side. Early talking and listening experiences translate over into the ability to read and write. At the same time, authentic reading and writing experiences enhance one's verbal and listening skill abilities (Strickland, 2012). Success in one literacy area supports success in the other literacy areas.

Instead of asking a majority of closed-ended and factual questions in class, or those that may require a "yes" or "no" answer, thinking and responding at more complex, creative, and deeper levels is crucially important for children. Factual based questions are important, but teachers will want to give children practice with higher level *open-ended* questions, making sure that *all* children have opportunities to give and share their individual responses and creative ideas. This is another way of *cultivating early reading development* and experiences so that children can move smoothly through the grades into later deeper levels of reading comprehension, solving real-life problems, and the joy of *reaping the benefits* of overall *school success* (Bay & Hartman, 2015; Ruddell, 2006; Wqlsh & Kemp, 2012).).

Reading comprehension is the act of making meaning from what one is reading. Comprehension is a complex process comprised of many different skills and strategies (Temple, Ogle, Crawford, & Freppon, 2014). Some components of reading comprehension include prior, or *background knowledge*, being able to *visualize* or see images as you read and *summarizing* the main idea of a section of text. To draw upon background knowledge, it helps to have applicable vocabulary to match what one already knows. Visualization is important when certain words conjure up meanings and images that can be seen in the reader's mind while reading. Regarding summarizing, proficient readers can identify and retell the important points in a particular passage of text. Reading widely increases vocabulary growth and comprehension (Pang, 2008; Temple et al., 2014).

Knowledge of words and the learning of new words has a strong impact on and is highly correlated with reading comprehension. Messages are made up of ideas that are expressed in words (Al-Darayseh, 2014). This need for the learning of new words pertains especially to students transitioning from primary grades into fourth grade, where there are fewer narrative storybook texts and more expository/informational textbooks. These expository textbooks have a heavy emphasis on complex scientific terms and other subject-matter vocabulary (Sanacore & Palumbo, 2009). *Targeted vocabulary instruction,* along with meaningful reading and writing activities, help students to *apply* new words that they have learned. A well-developed vocabulary aids in dealing with later more advanced vocabulary words and concepts in expository textbooks.

Academic success always looks good on you!

2 KEY EARLY FOUNDATION READING SKILLS

Phonemic awareness. Since *low* phonemic skill awareness (the awareness that words are made up of sounds, or phonemes) is the ***first obstacle*** for children in 1) word decoding, 2) spelling, and later on, 3) reading comprehension, *segmenting* and *blending* words, in the context of *meaningful* reading activities, are the **two** most **critical skills** for learning to read (Yopp, 1995; Patel, 2010). The English language is made up of consonants, vowels, and phonemes (the smallest units of speech sounds). Breaking apart or segmenting words into their individual phonemes can be problematic for many children who then have trouble with word reading. This can later lead to problems with fluency, spelling, comprehension, and overall reading development.

During the fourteenth through the sixteenth centuries, the way English vowels were pronounced changed, but the spellings of these words did not change. This can be very troublesome for young readers and second language learners when vowel sounds and their spellings do not match. What can be even more confusing is that regarding double vowel sounds (diphthongs), the spellings of some diphthong sounds match their spelling, while other diphthongs do not. Teachers can help by having a keen understanding of how English sounds are made and how English words are built in many different and unique ways (Temple et al., 2014).

The vowels and concepts that make up words are important to the study of how the brain measures development of these skills during infancy and beyond. The field of cognitive neuroscience refers to this process as *phonetic perception.* The role that experience and social interaction play in development of phonetic units of language, word learning, and reading is also crucial to the study of early language acquisition and overall childhood development (Kuhl, 2010; Wasserman, 2007).

Hruby & Goswami (2011) asserted that the act of reading is more than just mentally and verbally blending letters into words and comprehending text. Reading is a complex and contextual interaction between both cognitive and sociolinguistic/cultural factors. Sanders (2012) reported that Rosenblatt's reader response theory was a process of the reader constructing and creating meaning for text by combining text with his or her personal experiences. There is no single meaning for text. Readers bring multiple perspectives, interpretations, and various background experiences to the reading event (Brooks, & Hampton, 2005; Sanders, 2012).

The important role of reading fluency. There are four dimensions of reading fluency: 1) accurate and automatic word recognition, 2) efficient text reading at an appropriate speed,

3) meaningful voice inflection, and 4) meaningful grouping of words (Temple et al., 2014). Reading fluency is not just about reading fast. Reading fluency is a process that is more about a deep interconnected relationship between decoding skills and automatic and effortless reading that results in the enhancement of reading comprehension.

One strategy that has been shown to positively impact reading fluency is Readers Theatre. In Readers Theatre, children build their reading fluency skills by reading/performing for an audience a designated script, with expression that is meaningful. Thus, reading expression and meaning of text are improved with this process and participation in Readers Theatre (Young & Rasinski, 2009).

Phonics and phonemic awareness skills give children a *fast strategy* for decoding unfamiliar words, which usually leads to more *confident* reading and *increased fluency,* resulting in improved vocabulary development and reading comprehension. *Oral reading fluency* is associated with overall reading success (Crowe, Connor, & Petscher, 2009; Logan & Johnston, 2010). Reading fluency has a positive impact on academic achievement and school outcomes across school grades and content area subjects (Bgozzi, Tarchi, Vagnoli, Valente, & Pinto, 2017).

The reading failures of some struggling readers can be turned around with strategic interventions, but research has consistently shown that if a child is not reading proficiently by *age 8,* or by the *end of third grade,* he/she will more than likely struggle with reading through their grade school years (Dorn & Schubert, 2008; Menzies, Mahdavi, & Lewis, 2008).

Third-grade reading scores can predict a student's likelihood of dropping out of school long before high school graduation.

Thus, *the process of dropping out of school* may start as early as ***fourth grade.***

Although the outlook is not promising for children who are still not proficient in reading by the end of third grade, the National Institute of Child Health and Human Services reported that, "*treatment* intervention research has shown that appropriate *direct instruction* seems to be the best *medicine* for reading problems" (Grossen, 1997, p. 6).

Oh, that look of self-confidence!

3 UNDERSTANDING THE CONCEPT OF CURRICULUM AND INSTRUCTION

Curriculum is the content of *what* teachers teach and what students learn across subject areas. This includes the books, materials, and technology resources that teachers use with students. High-quality and effective curriculum should be central to: a) students' academic progress and assessment, b) a teacher's instructional practices, which have a significant impact on student achievement, and c) the interactions between teachers and students.

In our increasingly diverse school communities, high-quality and effective curriculum should also be central to students having access to positive reading materials and books, across subject matter areas, that are culturally relevant and those materials with which the students can identify (Goldman & Pellegrino, 2015; Kagan & Kauerz, 2012; Montgomery, 2001;Temple et al., 2014). Providing children with authentic, purposeful, and culturally relevant literature increases reader motivation, engagement, and opportunities for independent thinking (McLeod, 2012; Short, Lynch Brown, & Tomlinson, 2014). Children learn at a faster and more productive pace when they are working with culturally relevant materials that they are acquainted and familiar with (Cole, Hakkarainen, & Bredikyte, 2010).

It is very important that young children have the opportunity to participate and be actively involved in an early foundational reading program curriculum that has a focus on the development of strong oral language and phonemic awareness skills (Suggate, Schaughency, & Reese, 2012).

Instruction is *how* curriculum is taught. *Constructivist* instructional strategies are based on student engagement and active learning. Teachers use *scaffolding techniques*, or temporary support systems, where relevant task-steps are *modeled* for students. Teachers also *think out loud* when working through demonstration problems, or more difficult reading tasks, so that students can see what the problem solving thought process looks like. Students are given increasing responsibility, or *gradual release*, for engaging in the learning activity as their confidence and independent work skills increase. For example, teachers may use graphic organizers to help students organize their thoughts before participating in a learning activity.

Graphic organizers also help students to interpret their topic information and visualize relationships among concepts (Pang, 2009; Rosenshine, 2012). Students do better when they have a clear understanding of their learning expectations and what success looks like (Akhondi, Malayeri, & Samad, 2011;

Alfieri, Brooks, Aldrich, & Tenenbaum, 2011; Van Merrienboer, Kirschner, & Kester, 2003).

Daily independent student *practice* and *review* is an important dimension of instruction. This guided practice by the teacher should be full and adequate in preparing students to engage in *successful* practice so that they won't be practicing errors. With modeling and practice, *new material* to be learned should be *broken down* and presented in *small steps* or in small chunks, through lecture and/or demonstration/*worked examples*, asking questions, and checking for understanding. Ongoing opportunities for practice and review help students to further see connections and relationships among the concepts that they are learning and to be able to *transfer* these relationships over into new material that will be presented later in subsequent lessons (Rosenshine, 2012).

4 KINDERGARTEN, FIRST-, AND SECOND-GRADE READING INSTRUCTION

Explicit, systematic instruction. There is *explicit and systematic instruction* that focuses on the two key phonemic awareness skills: 1) *segmenting* words into their individual sounds, and 2) *blending* sounds together to make words. This instruction and student learning takes place in the context of real stories. These skills, which aid in comprehension, should be ongoing, embedded in, and connected to a *balanced/* holistic reading program at the preschool through primary grade levels (Yopp, 1995).

A balanced reading approach also includes instruction in making letter-sound associations, recognizing words by sight, word study instruction, vocabulary development activities, and instruction in comprehension strategies. There is a concentrated effort on using authentic/ meaningful reading materials for advancing and promoting students' language and comprehension skills. A balanced reading program is beneficial for all students (Logan & Johnston, 2010; Temple et al., 2014).

Decodable text. Instruction in phonemic awareness and letter-sound associations takes place, using decodable text, or words with sound-letter associations that the student has already been taught and knows how to sound out. Real stories are used that the children independently read or have read to them.

The use of decodable text gives children opportunities to practice *applying* letter-sound associations to *real stories* and balancing and *integrating* phonics into connected reading that is meaningful and captures the child's interest. Greater brain activity occurs in response to letters that are strung together into real words (Hruby & Goswami, 2011).

Reading development and achievement in beginning phonemic awareness skills in kindergarten have a *direct impact* on reading achievement in later grades. Thus, reading instruction and comprehension at kindergarten, first, and second grades refers to *direct and systematic instruction* in those prerequisite phonemic awareness skills and word recognition or *fluency* skills needed for success in "learning to read," skills which serve as a *bridge* to the *shift* to "reading to learn," at fourth grade and beyond (Sanacore & Palumbo, 2009, p. 67; Yopp, 1995).

The "switch-over" in first and second grades and beyond. Children are gradually able to switch over from concentration on word decoding and word identification skills (sight words) to a *focus* on **morphemes**—recognizing the meaning of word parts and syntax—sentence structure. This transition to the focus on meaning of word parts and how sentences are organized enables students to experience increased success in:1) making predictions, 2) visualizing images and seeing connections, 3) constructing meaning from text, and 4) understanding what they are reading (Fang, 2012; Ruddell, 2006; Temple et al., 2014).

Since meaningful word parts are encountered over a number of years, as children progress through the grades, analyzing morphemes may become more complex; this is especially true regarding compound words, plurals and verb tenses, and prefixes and suffixes. Students develop their skills in recognizing the meaning of word parts through explicit instruction in word structure and encouragement to read widely. Students can keep a word journal of their word study/word sorts activities for extended study and application.

At third/fourth grade and above, students can work on the history of words and identifying word families, or "reading words derived from other words" (Temple et al., 2014, p. 141). Students can practice identifying word parts and meanings from Latin and Greek and work in teams to research ancient word parts. Many English words are made up of ancient word parts, like *tele* (to, or at a distance) in the word *telemarket* (marketing, or selling something from a distance).

It is imperative that children be given explicit instruction in how words are built (morphology), including awareness of root words, word parts, and the history of words (etymology). Having this knowledge helps to increase and expand children's vocabularies and enables them to spell and read more words in context.

The joy of reading and sharing a book.

5 ASSESSMENT

Students' reading levels and progress should not be evaluated and determined solely, on the results of one end-of-the-year standardized test. In addition to the standardized test, formative or *authentic assessments* should be used, as they are an *ongoing* measurement of student progress through teacher daily observation of reading and literacy activities. The effective teacher sees how students' independent work habits and skill level are *fluid* and an *ongoing* process over time. Instruction is adjusted, as needed, to respond to individual student needs and improve student academic outcomes (Dorn & Schubert, 2008). Thus, assessment is viewed as a regular component and extension of instruction.

Giving students positive *timely feedback* and tools to self-monitor and become independent learners across subject areas can increase their self-confidence, motivation, student engagement, and overall reading achievement (Cauley & McMillan, 2010; Graham et al., 2013). Flexible instructional groups are used, where children can experience success and not be locked into a low reading group. Instructional practices have a substantial impact on student achievement. Thus, authentic assessment is a valuable tool for *guiding* instruction.

Authentic or formative assessments also work well for measuring the success of preschool programs. In addition, using authentic assessments in a preschool setting may have a positive influence on that early learning environment.

For example, Brenneman and Louro (2008) emphasized that conversing with preschool children about their science journals provides opportunities for both, assessing their understanding and informing further instruction. Like assessments for older students, early literacy assessments are key to guiding and informing instruction (Hallam, Grisham-Brown, Gao, & Brookshire, 2007). Contrary to one-time standardized testing procedures, this formative and authentic assessment process allows children to reveal their "expressions of understanding" in their daily classroom learning environment (Rushton, Juola-Rushton, & Larkin, 2009, p. 359).

6 THIRD-GRADE READING INSTRUCTION

The Third Grade Reading Program serves as a *bridge* between strengthening and extending students' early foundation primary grade phonemic awareness skills and fourth grade. Now in third grade, students should be getting a head start by engaging with an increased use of interesting information but more challenging texts. Children enter third grade with varying levels of early experiences and reading proficiency, depending on:

- whether or not they have had direct and ongoing phonemic awareness instruction in kindergarten, first, and second grades, alongside engagement with meaningful vocabulary and connected text and
- whether or not they have had early home and/or enriched preschool experiences, with opportunities to discuss and engage with a wide variety of books and advanced vocabulary and comprehension concepts.

Before getting to third grade, not all kindergarten and early primary grade children have been involved in a *balanced* reading program. A balanced reading program would include *both* direct and ongoing phonemic awareness skills instruction and engagement with *meaningful* and *connected* text that used rich vocabulary and real-life, interesting stories. Children should have also been studying word meanings (morphemes) and how sentences are organized (syntax).

From the beginning, children also need classroom libraries that are stocked with a variety of narrative text, along with an *increase* in exposure to *informational* and *expository text*. Early primary grade children will encounter these informational and expository textbooks on a more abstract and complex basis, especially in subjects, like social studies and scientific inquiry in the intermediate grades. Robinson et al. (2012) pointed out that content area subjects can provide a forum for students to practice their reading and writing skills.

Like at all grades, third grade reading assessment should be *authentic,* or an ongoing process of looking at student reading performance data and then adjusting instruction, as needed, to respond to individual student needs.

*Again, research has consistently informed us that if children are not reading proficiently by *age 8, or by the end of third grade,* they will more than likely struggle with reading at fourth grade and on up through other grades (Dorn & Schubert, 2008).

7 READING MOTIVATION IS KEY

Increased exposure to, and engagement of primary grade children with informational text will aid in building their background knowledge and developing their vocabulary and concepts in multiple subject content areas.

Worth (2010) reported that young children's curiosity about the world around them makes science a natural area for exploration and further learning. Through scientific inquiry, children can extend their foundational knowledge about science, enhance their basic skills in reading and math, and increase their ability to effectively communicate and work cooperatively together in groups. Increased exposure to informational text will also help primary-grade children to be better prepared for the demands of the more complex vocabulary and text structures of expository/informational textbooks that take place at around fourth grade and beyond.

Building student *self-confidence*, *interest*, and *value of reading* increases motivation (Fang, 2008; Sanacore &

Palumbo, 2009; Strickland, 2012). Enhanced feelings of competency and self-confidence *heighten motivation.* Motivation, in turn, results in gains in reading achievement and accomplishment of goals one is working toward (Dwek, 1999; Northouse, 2014). Thus, *motivation plays a critical role in the development of reading* (Marinak & Gambrell, 2010). When students are motivated to read, see a meaningful and authentic purpose for reading, and are self-confident about their reading, they are apt to become more positively engaged with text and reading activities. Children benefit from seeing a purpose for reading and how they can use it to do and accomplish other things (Daniels & Steres, 2011; Meth, 2010; Robinson et al., 2012.

Mindset plays an important role here. As opposed to a fixed mindset, a growth mindset is a belief that ability is not fixed, but fluid, and can be developed and improved by hard work and effort put into the process of successfully reaching an academic learning goal. Students will be *reaping the benefits* of *school success* as a direct result of this continued authentic *cultivating of early reading development* that is taking place in their learning environment. Timely *feedback* is provided that praises the process and effort that the student put into the successful accomplishment of the task. Going forward, challenges and setbacks are seen as opportunities to learn from one's mistakes and grow (Alfieri et al., 2011; Dweck, 1999; Dwek, 2006; Dweck, 2007; Karmins & Dweck, 1999; Pang, 2009).

Once you find interesting reading material, there's no stopping you!

8 FOURTH-GRADE TRANSITION

Children who have *not* had early *explicit and systematic instruction* in phonemic awareness and consistent engagement with a *wide variety of books* and more *advanced vocabulary*, struggle with the *shift* from "learning to read" in the primary grades to "reading to learn" at around fourth grade and beyond. Commonly known as the "fourth-grade slump," some students' reading motivation and scores begin to go down. (Sanacore & Palumbo, 2009, p. 68). This is especially true for students with learning disabilities, second- language learners, and children from low-income homes. Children from low-income homes most likely have not had the same kind of exposure to a wide variety of books and more advanced vocabulary, as children from higher socioeconomic homes. The more words a student knows, the easier it is to read and comprehend what is read. Higher socioeconomic parents usually have higher levels of education, income, and can afford more resources and experiences for their children (Biggam & Itterly, 2009; Hart & Risley, 1995; Lervag & Akrust, 2010; Ward Lonergan & Dutbie, 2016).

Expository subject-matter textbooks. Expository/informational textbooks have complex and difficult-to-navigate text structures that are loaded with intense abstract vocabulary and other scientific terms and concepts. Compared to the narrative storybook text that primary children had been accustomed to, these more challenging expository textbooks contain, what is referred to as "academic language." That is, the language is more abstract than and different from everyday language that children use in the context of their home relationships and daily lives (Demir, Rowe, Heller, Goldin Meadow, & Levine, 2015, p. 161; Fang, 2008).

Like the text and language of intermediate-grade expository/informational textbooks, the overall language of school is *decontextualized,* or more challenging and is also referred to as academic language. That is, the language of both intermediate informational subject-matter textbooks and the language of formal schooling, in general, is more abstract and different from the everyday language that children use at home and with their families.

The early use of decontextualized (academic) language by *parents* with their young children is a predictor of language skills at kindergarten entry. Regarding parent involvement in their child's preschool, Arnold, Zeljo, & Doctoroff (2008) found a direct correlation between increased parent home-school involvement and increased preliteracy skills of their children. Preliteracy skills refer to those early foundation skills, such as knowledge of the alphabet, phonics and phonemic awareness skills, word recognition and decoding skills, and listening comprehension of stories read to them. These

Stepping up to the challenge!

early skills serve as a bridge to formal school core reading instruction at kindergarten and/or first grade (Fischel, Braken, Fuchs-Eisenberg, Spira, Katz, & Shaller, 2007). The use of decontextualized language by parents with their children also has a positive impact on oral language development and preparing children for the more challenging/abstract vocabulary and complex language structures that takes place at formal school kindergarten entry and beyond (Demir, Rowe, Heller, Goldin-Meadow, & Levine, 2015, p. 161; Fang, 2008).

Expository textbook structures. Expository/informational textbooks have complex and difficult-to-navigate text structures. The five most commonly used expository textbook structures or text features are: 1) Description: a topic is described by the author, 2) Sequence: items/events listed in chronological order, 3) Compare/ Contrast: of two or more topics, items, events, 4) Cause/Effect: cause(s) noted, then effects described, and 5) Problem/Solution: problem is given then answered (Moss, 2004). These text structures tell the reader how the text is organized. *Signal words and phrases,* or cue words, are implied and prompt the reader as to which text structure they are encountering as they read. For example, in a chart of signal words and phrases, Masoumeh, Malayeri, & Samad (2011) identified three signal words for the text structure, sequence: "first," "next," and "later." A signal word and a signal phrase for the text structure, compare/contrast, are "similarly" and "on the other hand" (p. 370).

Students need to be taught proper and *specific strategies* in how to use graphic organizers to identify, organize, understand, and use these challenging intermediate grade level text structures. Authors use these text structures to arrange and connect ideas. Knowing how to identify and properly use *expository text structures* and the *signal words and phrases* that accompany the text structures enables students to see and understand relationships among the text ideas, adequately comprehend the material, and select the most important information for the task at hand. This results in improvement in both comprehension and overall reading achievement (Akhondi et al., 2011; Connor, Morrison, Jewkes, 2011; Fang, 2008; Hermida, 2009; Masoumeh et al., 2011).

Children should have access to both narrative storybooks and informational subject-matter books.

9 EIGHT-STEP PLAN FOR TEACHING EXPOSITORY TEXT STRUCTURES

Step 1. The five text structures: description, sequence, compare/contrast, cause/effect, and problem/solution should be introduced in the order given here, using signal words and phrases, such as (alike-different) for the compare/contrast structure (Akhondi et al., 2011).

Step 2. Students use informational books to practice and work on one text strategy, along with their signal words and phrases, for each lesson.

Step 3. The embedded writing instruction comes in here as students are given time to practice writing paragraphs, using the text structure they are working on at that time.

Step 4. Teacher models and points out various signal words and phrases in the text. For example, the words—next, following, subsequently, prior to—would be highlighted and discussed as belonging with the text structure of sequence.

Step 5. As students become familiar and comfortable with the process, they practice picking out signal words and phrases from the text.

Step 6. Embedded organization and writing comes in here again, as students are ready to view a completed *graphic organizer* as a model of what a planned paragraph looks like.

Step 7. Students then progress to finishing an incomplete graphic organizer on their own. They have been gradually released to full independence.

Step 8. In this final step, a blank graphic organizer is used to retrieve the most important information from the text to transfer into the applicable areas of the graphic organizer. Teaching reading through text structures improves reading comprehension.

10 TEACHING ENGLISH LANGUAGE LEARNERS

Two key principles for teaching English Language Learners (ELLs):

1) Realize that social interaction enhances both the conversational and academic language skills of ELLs.
2) English language learners benefit from learning activities and classroom environments that minimize stress about learning English.

English oral language and vocabulary skills. ELLs start school with a more advanced listening comprehension compared to their English-speaking skills, so there should be a focus on developing their *English oral language* and *vocabulary* skills (Robinson, et al., 2012; Temple et al., 2014). For very young preschool-aged children, Markova (2016) found that second-language learners interacted more with others during free-play activities. This gave the ELL children more opportunities to practice and gain more proficiency in their English-speaking skills. Socially situated and playful learning activities provided a meaningful

The library has an unlimited number of reading and education resources.

context for preschool ELL children to use their developing English skills.

Lucas, Villegas, and Freedson-Gonzalez (2008) asserted that social interaction enhances both the conversational and academic language skills of ELLs. Rushton (2011) further emphasized that, even for primarily English-speaking preschool children, playful learning allows for mastering concepts and reaching learning goals across a variety of subject areas. Lucas et al. (2008) described six strategies for developing the oral language and vocabulary skills of ELLs:

1. For very young children, use **pictures**, **objects**, and **puppets** to teach nouns and other action word *vocabulary*.

2. Use **open-ended questions.** They provide ELL students with opportunities to use higher levels of thinking to practice, express, and use their developing *oral language skills* in English. Example: Please tell me what you know about_____?

3. **Reading aloud to groups of children.** Groups that contain both English speakers and English learners give ELLs an opportunity to *interact* with other students and see good reading habits modeled by the teacher. They also have opportunities to hear and **discuss** new *vocabulary* words being presented from **good books.** *Remember, ELL children start school with a more advanced listening comprehension compared to their English-speaking skills. Thus, read-alouds are important for helping them understand more complex text.

4. For independent reading, use *meaningful* and *interesting* **decodable text** for further practice in *applying* their decoding skills for continued development of their sight word and automatic word recognition skills in the context of *real stories.*

5. **Teach, explicitly, word meanings and phrases,** especially those more complex and abstract technical academic terms and phrases found in subject-matter expository textbooks at around fourth grade.

6. **Comprehension monitoring.** When teaching comprehension, teach ELLs how to monitor their comprehension by having them use *fix-up strategies*: reread, get picture clues, figure out and apply word-part meanings (Lucas, et al., 2008).

11 CHILDREN WITH LEARNING DISABILITIES

Some children struggling with reading may have a *specific learning disability* in reading. Since these disabilities are often overlooked and not diagnosed for long periods of time, *early identification* is critical for *prevention, intervention,* and academic *special treatments* as early as possible. The Individuals With Disabilities Education Act (IDEA) is a federal law that mandates inclusive public education services for students with specific learning disabilities. Each eligible child is required to have an Individualized Educational Program (IEP), which outlines his/her detailed educational service needs that will be received. Parents must be included on the IEP team. The education services for special needs children should take place in the "least restrictive environment," as much as possible, with children in the regular education program (Lipkin & Okamoto, 2015, p. 1651).

The Response to Intervention (RTI) model is used, where the entire class is given a series of *screening tests* to identify who will need further extra reading assistance in the

RTI program. The focus is on student outcomes on leveled/tiered specific treatment practice exercises. The reading outcomes of children identified for needing extra reading help are matched with specific tiered areas of reading dimension exercises for assessment, called *"progress-monitoring"* assessment. The outcomes of these assessments reflect the ongoing monitoring and assessment of those specific treatment exercises over time (Guralnick, 2017; Pesovq, Sivevska, & Runceva, 2014; Lipkin & Okamoto, 2015; McCormick, & Zutell, 2015, p. 96).

12 CONCLUSION

The ability to decode, read, and comprehend written text is one of the most critical skills that children can develop. Reading not only increases one's knowledge about the world around them, but more importantly, reading enables students to be successful in other content subject areas and use their skills to enhance their everyday lives (Alvermann, Gillis, & Phelps, 2013; Temple et al., 2014). It is the task of the teacher to, not only know the various components of reading ability, but teachers should also understand how to use a variety of instructional strategies and materials to meet the diverse and multicultural needs of their students.

The encouraging news is that, although the brain experiences its most critical growth during the first three years of life, the brain continues to grow and develop throughout one's lifetime. Therefore, *high- quality preschool programs* and *instruction and interventions* throughout the primary grades and beyond provide an early critical advantage for helping to make up for some and/or all of the losses of children who

Reading Success: We are all in this together!

have had a less than sufficient start in content area, word knowledge, and vocabulary development (Omrod, 2016; Sanacore & Palumbo, 2009). However, Wasserman (2007) emphasized that the best window of opportunity for all language learning generally takes place from birth through age ten.

Three overall critical parental influences on children's school adjustment are: 1) early meaningful home reading experiences, 2) consistent and meaningful parent-child interactions, and 3) high parental expectations. Thus, early nurture and social relationships play a key role in home and school learning (Lunenburg, 2011; Mustard, 2010). However, early childhood educators must realize that a child's development does not progress along a linear or universal pathway. Childhood development, from a cultural psychology perspective, is a systemic process. This systemic process takes place not only in the school context but in the context of the home, the extended family, and the community at large (Lee & Johnson, 2007).

Community resources can be incorporated into the classroom curriculum. Therefore, teachers must, through culturally responsive classrooms and curriculum, get to know their diverse student populations and their various interests and learning styles. Instructional approaches, materials, and learning tasks are matched to students' backgrounds and needs so that students find meaning, purpose, and connection to their out-of-school learning contexts (Lee & Johnson, 2007; Montgomery, 2001).

Cultivating the *early reading development* and literacy experiences of young children gives them a better chance at *reaping the benefits* of increased academic achievement outcomes, positive self-regulation skills, and ongoing *school success.* Brown (2014)

Access to technology is a valuable tool for extending learning and educational/career opportunities!

maintained that reading is a comprehensive and continuing process that includes a wide variety of developmental skills and competencies. Optimum efforts and opportunities for authentic early reading development are critically urgent if young children are to experience the benefits of ongoing progress and success in their early and subsequent years of schooling.

Access to preschool and other early literacy experiences continues to be an increasing global phenomenon. Between 1990 and 2014, there is evidence of a 16% increase in preschool enrollment around the world. The reality of school readiness is that it encompasses a seamless and comprehensive set of skills that include development in language and literacy, knowledge, and appropriate proficiency across content subject areas, and age-appropriate development in social-emotional and self-regulation skills (Rimm Kaufman & Sandilos, 2017). "Adequate reading comprehension skills are crucial for virtually all aspects of formal education, as well as for full participation in society" (Lervag & Aukrust, 2010, p. 612).

ABOUT THE AUTHOR

After 34 years of teaching at the elementary and middle school levels (CA), retirement, and WHILE going through cancer (2007), Alvin started Haywood's Reading-Language Clinic in his garage! He stopped long enough to go in for 28 days of radiation therapy and, three months later, he was declared cancer-free! Alvin went on to earn his doctorate degree in Education, with a Concentration in Reading Education, through Nova Southeastern University (FL). Dr. Alvin Haywood, Ed.D., received BA degrees in Social Work and Psychology, an MA degree in Education, and both Teaching and Administrative credentials from San Jose State University (CA).

As Dr. Haywood continues on as an Educational Consultant, Haywood's Reading/Language Clinic has become a "traveling" consultancy agency as Alvin is a member of the Public Policy Committee and the Legislative Action Workgroup of the California Association for the Education of Young Children (CAAEYC). This Legislative Action Workgroup reviews early education and childcare legislation to determine their impact on young children, and then advises the CAAEYC on whether to support or oppose these legislative bills. Dr. Haywood is also a member of the American Educational Research Association (AERA) and the Education Law Association (ELA).

The ELA is a national organization that stimulates dialogue and the sharing of stories between educators and attorneys about legal issues in education.

Good reading experiences make you feel like you're on top of the world!

REFERENCES

Akhondi, M., Malayeri, F. A., & Samad, A. A. (2011). How to teach expository text structure to facilitate reading comprehension. *The Reading Teacher, 64*(5), 368-371.

Alfieri, L., Brooks, P. J., Aldrich, N. J., & Tenenbaum, H. R. (2011). Does discovery based instruction enhance learning? *Journal of Educational Psychology, 103*(1), 1-18.

Anderson, P. J., & Reidy, N. (2012). Assessing executive function in preschoolers. *Neuropsychology Review, 22*, 345-360. Doi: 10.1007/s1065-012-9220-3

Bakken, L., Brown, N., & Downing, B. (2017). Early childhood education: The long-term benefits. *Journal of Research in Childhood Education, 31*(2), 255-269.

Bay, D. N., & Hartman, D. K. (2012). Teachers askingin preschool. *International Journal of Humanities and Social Science, 7*(1), 60-76.

Bgozzi, L., Tarchi. C., Vagnoli, L., Valente, E., & Pinto, G. (2017). Reading fluency as a predictor of school outcomes across grades, 4-9. doi:10.3389/psyg.201700200

Brenneman, K., & Louro, I. F. (2008). Science journals in the preschool classroom. *Early Childhood Education Journal, 36,* 113-119.

Biggam, S., & Itterly, K. (2009). *Literacy profiles: A framework to guide assessment,instructional strategies and intervention, K-4,* NY: Allyn and Bacon.

Brooks, W., & Hampton, G. (2005). Safe discussions rather than first hand encounters: Adolescents examine racism through one historical fiction text. *Children's Literature in Education, 36,*(1), 83-98.

Brown, C. S. (2014). Language and literacy development in the early years: Foundational skills that support emergent readers. *The Language and Literacy Spectrum, 24,* 35-49.

Bursuck, W. D., & Damer, M. (2007). *Teaching reading to students who are at risk or have disabilities* (3rd ed.). Boston, MA: Pearson.

Cascio, E. U., & Schanzenbach, D. W. (2013). The impacts of expanding access to high quality preschool education. Brookings Papers on Economic Activity. Northwestern University. Retrieved from http://www.brookings.edu

Cole, M., Hakkarainen, P., & Bredikyte, M. (2010). Culture and early childhood learning. *Encyclopedia on Early childhood Development*, 1-6.

Connor, C. M., Morrison, F. J., & Jewkes, A. M. (2011). Schooling effects on preschoolers' self-regulation, early literacy, and language growth. *Early Childhood Research Quarterly, 26*(1), 42-49.

Crowe, E. C., Connor, C. M., & Petscher, Y. (2009). Examining the core: Relations among reading curricula, poverty, and first through third grade reading achievement. *Journal of School Psychology, 47,* 108-214.

Cunningham, D. D. (2008). Literacy environment quality in preschool and children's attitudes toward reading and writing. *Literacy Teaching and Learning, 12,* 19-36.

Daniels, E., & Steres, M. (2011). Examining the effects of a school-wide reading culture on the engagement of middle school students. *Research in Middle Level Education, 35*(2), 1-13.

Demir, O. E., Rowe, M. L., Heller, G., Goldin-Meadow, S., & Levine, S. C. (2015). Vocabulary, syntax, and narrative development in typically developing children and children with early unilateral brain injury: Early parental talk about the "There-and-Then" matters. *Developmental Psychology, 51*(2), 161-175.

Dominguez, X., Vitiello, V. E., Fuccillo, J. M., Greenfield, D. B., & Bulotsky-Shearer, R. J. (2011). The role of context in preschool learning: A multilevel examination of the contribution of context-specific problem behaviors and classroom process quality to low-income children's approaches to learning. *Journal of School Psychology, 49*, 175-195.

Dorn, L., & Schubert, B. (2008). A comprehensive intervention model for preventing reading failure: A response to intervention process. *Journal of Reading Recovery, 7*(2), 29-41.

Dweck, C. S. (1999). *Self-theories: Their role in motivation, personality, and development.* Philadelphia, PA: Psychology Press.

Dwek, C. S. (2006). *Mindset: The new psychology of success.* New York, NY: Random House.

Dweck, C. S. (2007). Boosting achievement with messages that motivate. *Education Canada, 47*(2), 6-10. Retrieved from http://www.cea-ace.ca

Fang, Z. (2008). Going beyond the fab five: Helping students cope with the unique linguistic challenges of expository reading in intermediate grades. *Journal of Adolescent & Adult Literacy, 51*(8), 478-487.

Fang, Z. (2012). Approaches to developing content area literacies. *Journal of Adolescent & Adult Literacy, 56*, 103-108.

Goldman, S. R., & Pellegrino, J. W. (2015). Research on learning and instruction: Implications for curriculum , instruction, and assessment. *Policy Insights from the Behavioral and Brain Sciences, 2*(1), 31-41.

Gormley, W. T., Phillips, D., & Anderson, S. (2017). The effects of Tulsa's pre-k program on middle school student performance. *Journal of Policy Analysis and Management, 00*(0), 1-25. doi:10.2/pam.22023

Graham, S., & Hebert, M. (2011). Writing to read: A meta-analysis of the impact of Writing and writing instruction on reading. *Harvard Educational Review, 81*(4), 710-744.

Graham, S., MacArthur, C. A., & Fitzgerald, J. (2013). *Best practices in writing instruction* (2nd ed.). New York, NY: The Guilford Press.

Grossen, B. (1997). A synthesis of research on reading conducted by the National Institute of Child Health and Human Development.

Guralnick, M. J. (2017). Early interventions for children with intellectual disabilities: An update. *Journal of Applied Research in Intellectual Disabilities, 30,* 211-229.

Hallam, R., Grisham-Brown, J., Gao, X., & Brookshire, R. (2007). The effects of outcomes-driven authentic assessment on classroom quality. *Early Childhood Research & Practice, 9*(3), Retrieved from http://ecrp.uluc.edu

Hart, B., & Risley, T. (1995). *Meaningful differences in the everyday experience of young American children.* Baltimore, MD: Brookes. Baltimore, MD: Brookes.

Hermida, J. (2009). The importance of teaching academic reading skills in first-year university courses. *The International journal of Research and Review, 3,* 20-30.

Hruby, G. G., & Goswami, U. (2011). Neuroscience and reading: A review for reading education researchers. *Reading Research Quarterly, 46*(2), 156-172.

International Reading Association Common Core State Standards (CCSS) Committee, 2012. Literacy implementation guidance for the ELA Common Core State Standards. Retrieved from ttp://www.reading.org

Justice, L. M. (2006). Evidence-based practice, response to intervention, and the prevention of reading difficulties. *Language, Speech, and Hearing Services in Schools, 37,* 244-297.

Kagan, S. L., & Kauerz, K. (2012). Preschool programs.: Effective curricula. *Encyclopedia on Early Childhood Development,* 1-4. Retrieved from http://www.child-encyclopedia.com

Karmins, K. L., & Dweck, C. S. (1999). Person versus process praise and criticism: Implications for contingent self-worth and coping. *Developmental Psychology, 35,* 835-847.

Karoly, L. (2017). The economic returns from investing in early childhood programs in the granite. RAND Corporation. doi:10.7249/RB-9952-EH

Kuhl, P. K. (2010). Brain mechanisms in early language acquisition. *Neuron, 67*(5), 713-727.

Kupcha-Szrom, J. (2011). A window to the world: Early language and literacy development. *Zero To three Policy Center.* Retrieved from http://www.zerotothree.org

Lee, K., & Johnson, A. S. (2007). Childhood development in cultural contexts: Implications of cultural psychology for early childhood teacher education. *Early Education Journal, 35,* 233-243.

Lervag, A., & Aukrust, V. G. (2010). Vocabulary development is a critical determinant of the difference in reading comprehension growth between first and second language learners. *The Journal of Child Psychology and Child Psychiatry, 51*(5), 612-620.

Lipkin, P. N., & Okamoto, J. (2015). The Individual With Disabilities Education Act (IDEA) for children with special needs. *American Academy of Pediatrics,* 1650-1662. doi: 10.1542/peds.2015-5409

Logan, S., & Johnston, R. (2010). Investigating gender differences in reading. *Education Review, 62*(2), 175-187.

Lucas, T., Villegas, A. M., & Freedson,-Gonzalez, M. (2008). Linguistically responsive teacher education: Preparing classroom teachers to teach English language learners. *Journal of Teacher Education, 59*(11), 361-373.

Lunenburg, F. C. (2011). Early childhood education: Implications for school Readiness. *Schooling, 2*(1). 1-8.

Marinak, B., & Gambrell, L. (2010). Reading motivation: Exploring the elementary gender gap. *Literacy Research and Instruction, 49,* 129-141.

Markova, I. (2016). Effects of academic and non-academic instructional approaches on preschool English language learners' classroom engagement and English-language development. *Journal of Early Childhood Research, 15*(4), 339-358.

Masoumeh, A., Malayeri, F. A., & Samad, A. A. (2011). How to teach expository text structure to facilitate reading comprehension. *The Reading Teacher, 64*(5), 368-372.

McCormick, S., & Zutell, J. (2015). *Instructing students who have literacy problems* (7th ed.).. Boston, MA: Pearson.

McKeown, M. G., Beck, I. C., & Blake, R. G. K. (2009). Rethinking reading comprehension instruction: A comparison of instruction for strategies content approaches. *Reading Research Quarterly, 44*(3), 218-253.

McLeod, S. (2012). Bruner. Retrieved from http://www.simplypsychology.org

Menzies, H. M., Mahdavi, J. N., & Lewis, J. L. (2008). Early intervention in reading: From research to practice. *Remedial and Special Education, 29*(2), 67-77.

Meth, J. M. (2010). Inspiring curiosity and enthusiasm for nonfiction: A project designed to boost students' will to read. *English Journal, High School Edition, 100*(1), 76-82.

Montgomery, W. (2001). Creating culturally responsive, inclusive classrooms. *Teaching Exceptional Children, 33*(4), 4-9.

Mustard, J. F. (2010). Early brain development and human development. Retrieved from http://www.childhood-encyclopedia.com

Nespeca, S. M. (2012). The importance of play, particularly constructive play in public library programming. A white paper written for the Association for Library Services to Children. Retrieved from http://www.ala.org

Northouse, P. G. (2015). *Introduction to leadership: Concepts and practice* (3rd ed.).Los Angeles, CA: Sage.

Pang, K. (2009). An examination of constructivist-driven instructional design and its pedagogical implications for effective learning. *Transformative Dialogues: Teaching & Learning Journal, 3*(2), 1-9.

Patel, S. (2010). Reading at risk: Why effective literacy practice is not effective. *Waikato Journal of Education, 15*(3), 51-68.

Pesova, B., Sivevska, D., & Runceva, J. (2014). Early intervention and prevention of students with specific learning disabilities. *Procedia-Social and Behavioral Sciences, 149,* 701-708.

Reeves, D. (2015). 7 ways to increase a student's attention span. George Lucas Educational Foundation. Edutopia.

Reynolds,, A. J., & Temple, J. A. (2008). Cost-effective early childhood development programs from preschool to third grade.

Annual Review of Clinical Psychology, 4(109).doi.org/10.1146/annurev.clinpsy.3022806.091411

Rimm-Kaufman, S., & Sandilos, L. (2017). School transition and school readiness: An outcome of early childhood development. *Encyclopedia on Early Childhood Development.* Retrieved from http://www.child-encyclopedia.com

R. D., McKenna, M. & Conradi, K. (2012). *Issues and trends in literacy education.* Boston, MA: Pearson.

Rosenshine, B. (2012). Principles of instruction: Research-based strategies that all teachers should know. *American Educator, 36,*(1), 12-20. Retrieved from http://www.aft.org

Ruddell, R. B. (2006). *Teaching children to read and write: Becoming an effective literacy teacher* (4th ed.). Boston, MA: Pearson.

Rushton, S. (2011). Neuroscience, early childhood education and play: We are doing It right! *Early Childhood Education Journal, 39*(2), 89-94.

Rushton, S., Juola-Rushton, A., & Larkin, E. (2009). Neuroscience, play and early childhood education: Connections, implications and assessment. *Early Childhood Education Journal, 37,* 351-361.

Sanders, A. (2012). Rosenblatt's presence in the new literacies research. *National Council of Teachers of English, 24,* 1-6.

Short, K. G., Lynch-Brown, & Tomlinson, C. M. (2014). *Essentials of Children's Literature* (8th ed.). Upper Saddle River, NJ: Pearson.

Skolnick, D. S. Hirsh-Pasek, K., & Golinkoff, R. M. (2013). Guided play: Where curricular goals meet a pedagogy. *International Mind,Brain, and Education Society, 7*(2), 104-112.

Strickland, D. S. (2012). Planning curriculum to meet Common Core State Standards. *Reading Today, 29*(4), 25-26.

Suggate, S. P., Schaughency, E. A., & Reese, E. (2012). Children learning to read later Catch up to children reading earlier. *Early Childhook Research Quarterly, 28*(1), 33-48.

Sussman, K. S. (2012). The importance of play in the preschool classroom. *Texas childcare Quarterly, 36*(3), 1-8.

Temple, C., Ogle, D., Crawford, A., & Freppon, P. (2014). *All children read: Teaching for literacy in today's diverse classrooms* (4th ed.). Upper Saddle River, NJ: Pearson.

Van Merrienboer, J. J., Kirschner, P. A., & Kester, L. (2003). Taking the load off a learner's mind: Instructional design for complex learning. *Educational Psychologist, 38*(1), 5-13.

Walsh, R. L., & Kemp, C. R. (2012). Evaluating interventions for young gifted children Using single-subject methodology a preliminary study. *Gifted Child Quarterly*. doi: 10.1177/0016986212466259

Ward-Lonergan, J. M., & Dutbie, J. K. (2016). Intervention to improve expository reading comprehension skills in older children and adolescents with language disorders. *Top Language disorders, 36*(1), 52-64.

Wasserman, L. H. (2007). The correlation between brain development, language acquisition, and cognition. *Early Childhood Education Journal, 34*(6), 415-418.

Yopp, H. K. (1995). A test for assessing phonemic awareness in young children. *The Reading Teacher, 49*(1), 20-28.

Young, C., & Rasinski, T. (2009). Implementing readers theatre as an approach to classroom fluency instruction. *The Reading Teacher, 63*(1), 4-13.

Lightning Source UK Ltd.
Milton Keynes UK
UKHW021045081221
395259UK00006B/285